Healthy Kids Cookbook

100% Kid Approved Recipes

At Healthy Steps Nutrition, we focus on a simple, habit-based approach to empower families to **make health a way of life one step at a time!**

Thank you for taking the first step and investing in yourself by diving into this cookbook.

We have special bonuses just for you:
- Free Downloadable Guide: Family Nutrition Made Easy
- 4 Week Jumpstart: Nutrition Tips & Sample Meal Ideas
- Tips For Picky Eaters

To access these amazing bonuses, go to healthystepsnutrition.com/cookbook

Nicole Marchand Aucoin, RD
with Brody & Cooper Aucoin

ISBN: 9798675425761

Designed by Tessa Voccola
Photography by Pamella Falcao with Aludra Photography

Contents

Breakfast

Main Dishes

Sides

Treats

Snacks

Healthy Steps Nutrition Resources

The Story Behind
The Cookbook

While sitting at the dinner table one night, Nicole and Jason were talking to their kids, Brody and Cooper, about how to start a business. Nicole and Jason own a few businesses, including a CrossFit affiliate, a nutrition coaching company, and a mentoring company helping gym owners implement nutrition programs. The kids have seen what goes into owning businesses all their lives. Nicole said, "A successful business solves a problem."

The discussion led to a conversation about what problems they could solve. Cooper has always been a helper. She said, "What if we help kids eat healthier?" Within a few minutes, we had the drawing board out and were planning their kid's cookbook. Brody and Cooper have grown up eating healthy their entire life. They grew up in a blended household where both families focus on healthy habits and eating real foods.

There is a tribe of four parents and grandparents who have the privilege of raising these amazing little humans. This cookbook was the perfect opportunity to teach them how to start a business of their own. They worked hard to pick all of the cookbooks' recipes to inspire kids to eat healthy and get involved in the kitchen!

Here's a little note from them:

I hope you love all of my favorite recipes!

Love Brody

Cooking is so much fun. I hope you enjoy cooking as much as I do.

love Cooper

Breakfast

Amish Oatmeal

 Prep Time: 5 Minutes

 Cook Time: 25 Minutes

 Total Time: 30 Minutes

Servings: 10

Dietitian Pro Tip:

Instead of grabbing the "kids" oatmeal box loaded with sugar and low in protein, try this one! It's a great source of protein from the egg whites! Top it with your favorite fruit to make it your own.

Ingredients

- 1 cup old fashioned oats
- 1 cup quick quaker oats
- 3 tbsps light nectar agave
- 2/3 cup unsweetened almond milk
- 3 tbsps grass-fed butter
- 1 cup egg whites
- 1 egg
- 1/2 tsp salt
- 2 tsps vanilla extract

Instructions

1. Preheat oven to 350 °F and grease 13x9 pan with coconut oil

2. Combine all ingredients (oats, agave, melted butter, egg whites, salt, almond milk and vanilla extract) in a large mixing bowl

3. Stir well then pour into greased pan

4. Bake for 25-30 minutes or until edges are golden brown

5. Let cool then break up into little crumbles

6. Optional: top with warm almond milk, 2 tsp almond slivers and berries (not included in nutrition facts)

Nutrition Information Per Serving

Calories: 140, Total Fat: 6g, Total Carbohydrates: 17g, Protein: 6g

Cooper's Favorite

Egg Muffins

 Prep Time:
10 Minutes

 Cook Time:
18 Minutes

 Total Time:
28 Minutes

Servings:
10

Dietitian Pro Tip:

These little egg cups are a great added source of protein to your breakfast! Are you looking to change up the flavor? Mix in your favorite veggies and breakfast meats (for extra protein). Pair with fruit or greek yogurt for a balanced breakfast.

Ingredients

- 5 eggs
- 5 egg whites
- 1/2 cup onion diced
- 1 cup mushrooms diced

- 1/2 cup bell peppers diced
- 1 handful spinach
- 1 cup broccoli diced
- 3/4 cup ham

Instructions

1. Preheat oven to 350 °F

2. Dice up all vegetables

3. In a large mixing bowl, whisk eggs then add in all the diced vegetables and ham

4. Pour mixture in greased muffin pan (should fill about 10 muffins)

5. Bake for 18-20 minutes or until toothpick inserted in the middle comes out clean

Nutrition Information Per Serving

Calories: 100, Total Fat: 5g, Total Carbohydrates: 3g, Protein: 10g

Brody's Favorite

Sweet Potato Hash Egg Muffin

 Prep Time:
15 Minutes

 Cook Time:
50 Minutes

 Total Time:
1 hour 5 Minutes

Servings:
6

Dietitian Pro Tip:

Sweet potato egg muffins are the perfect balance of healthy carbohydrates, protein, and fat. Plus, you are getting in some veggies with breakfast!

Ingredients

- 1 small sweet potato
- 2 eggs
- 2 egg whites
- 1/2 tsp olive oil
- 2 slices turkey bacon chopped
- 1/2 red bell pepper chopped
- 1/4 yellow onion chopped
- seasonings (to taste) salt, pepper, garlic

Instructions

1. Preheat oven to 350 °F

2. Use a grater to shred sweet potato

3. Combine shredded sweet potato, olive oil, & seasonings

4. Spoon into sprayed muffin tin filling 6 muffin tins & bake for 30 mins

5. Combine eggs, turkey bacon, peppers, onion, & season

6. Pour egg mixture into baked sweet potato and continue to bake for 15-20 mins until eggs are cooked

Nutrition Information Per Serving

Calories: 100, Total Fat: 5g, Total Carbohydrates: 3g, Protein: 10g

Strawberries and Cream Steel-Cut Oats

 Prep Time:
5 Minutes

 Cook Time:
5 Hours

 Total Time:
5 Hours
5 Minutes

 Servings:
1

Dietitian Pro Tip:

We love making oatmeal and steel-cut oats because they are loaded with fiber, which will keep you full longer and keep you regular. Many of the prepackaged oatmeals are loaded with added sugar; instead, make it at home to control how much added sugar is in your breakfast! This steel-cut oats recipe is great because you can set it and forget it! Make it your own by topping it with your favorite nuts and fruit.

Ingredients

- 1 cup steel-cut oats
- 3 1/2 cups unsweetened almond milk
- 1 cup egg whites
- 2 scoops Bub's Natural Collagen
- 1 tsp vanilla extract
- 1 tsp cinnamon
- 1/3 cup half and half
- 2-3 sliced strawberries

Instructions

1. Place steel-cut oats in crockpot
2. Mix almond milk, egg whites and collagen powder in a bowl
3. Add liquid ingredients into the crockpot
4. Cook for 4 hours on low
5. Stir and add 1 tsp of vanilla extract and 1 tsp cinnamon
6. Cook for one more hour on low
7. Stir in strawberries and ⅓ cup cream

Nutrition Information Per Serving

Calories: 261, Total Fat: 7g, Total Carbohydrates: 31g, Protein: 17g

Protein Waffles with Strawberries

 Prep Time: 10 Minutes

 Cook Time: 5 Minutes

 Total Time: 15 Minutes

 Servings: 2

Dietitian Pro Tip:

Fun Fact: this recipe makes excellent waffles or pancakes! They are packed full of protein and a hit with the kids! Top with your favorite fruit.

Ingredients

- 3 tbsps unsweetened applesauce
- 1 egg
- 2 egg whites
- 3/4 cup old fashioned oats
- 1 scoop Ascent vanilla protein powder
- 1/2 tsp vanilla extract **optional
- 1/2 tsp cinnamon **optional
- 2 sliced strawberries

Breakfast

Instructions

1. Beat eggs and egg whites

2. Mix in applesauce, cinnamon, vanilla, oats and protein powder

3. Place 1/2 batter in waffle maker

4. Top with strawberries

6. Optional: top with 1 tsp almond butter (not included in nutrition facts label)

Nutrition Information Per Serving

Calories: 200, Total Fat: 5g, Total Carbohydrates: 24g, Protein: 16g

Greek Yogurt Parfait

Total Time:
5 Minutes

Servings:
1

Dietitian Pro Tip:

Greek yogurt is an excellent source of protein. To make it a balanced snack, add your favorite fruits and nuts on top. Be mindful, yogurt is often a hidden source of sugar! One of our favorite options is Chobani - less sugar madagascar vanilla & cinnamon.

Instructions

1. Start with your base.

Low sugar greek yogurt

2. Layer in 2 tablespoons of your favorite fruit

Strawberries

Blueberries

Raspberries

3. Add 1/2 teaspoon your favorite nuts

Walnuts

Pecans

Slivered Almonds

4. Sprinkle your favorite flavor like cinnamon or pumpkin spice on top

Cinnamon

Pumpkin Spice

5. Enjoy and try different combos

Nutrition Information Per Serving

Nutrition facts varies based on favorite fruit/nuts

Double Chocolate Overnight Oats

Prep Time:	Refrigerate:	Total Time:	Servings:
10 Minutes	8 Hours	8 Hours 10 Minutes	1

Dietitian Pro Tip:

Do you struggle to find time to make breakfast some mornings? This recipe is the perfect option for you! Prepare this delicious option the night before and just grab-n-go the next day.

Ingredients

- 1/2 scoop Chocolate Ascent Protein Powder
- 1/2 cup low sugar vanilla greek yogurt
- 1/3-1/2 cup unsweetened almond milk
- 1 tbsp dark chocolate chips
- 1/3 cup old fashioned oats
- 1 tbsp chia seeds

Instructions

1. Mix all ingredients together
2. Pour into mason jar
3. Store overnight in the refrigerator
4. Enjoy in the morning

Nutrition Information Per Serving

Calories: 340, Total Fat: 11g, Total Carbohydrates: 35g, Protein: 26g

Egg and Ham Cups

 Prep Time:
10 Minutes

 Cook Time:
20 Minutes

 Total Time:
30 Minutes

Servings:
8

Dietitian Pro Tip:

Egg and ham cups are a fun recipe to get the kids involved in the kitchen! These are a great option to prep on the weekend and reheat throughout the week for an on-the-go breakfast option!

Ingredients

- 8 Slices of Ham
- 8 Medium Eggs
- 1/3 cup Mozzerella Cheese
- 1 Basil leaf
- Salt & Pepper
- 8 Grape tomatoes

Instructions

1. Preheat oven to 350 °F
2. Wipe muffin tin with olive oil (to prevent from sticking)
3. Gently line each muffin cup with one slice of ham, you may cut the excess
4. Sprinkle cheese in ham-lined muffin cup
5. Break egg in a measuring cup and slide egg into the muffin cup (recommend medium eggs because large eggs will overflow)
6. Repeat for all muffin cups
7. Sprinkle with salt and pepper
8. Cut grape tomatoes in half and cut the basil leaf into small pieces

9. Top each muffin cup with 2 tomato haves and basil

10. Bake for 20 minutes on 350 °F

11. Let sit for 3 minutes then remove from the muffin cup

Nutrition Information Per Serving

Calories: 113, Total Fat: 7g, Total Carbohydrates: 1g, Protein: 11g

English Muffin Sandwich

 Prep Time:
5 Minutes

 Cook Time:
5 Minutes

Total Time:
10 Minutes

Servings:
1

Dietitian Pro Tip:

Who doesn't love a yummy breakfast sandwich? Make it your own by adding your favorite breakfast protein (Canadian bacon, ham, or turkey sausage). Bonus - they can be frozen and reheated in the microwave.

Ingredients

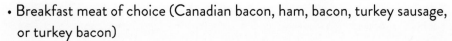

- Whole wheat english muffin
- 1 large egg
- 1 slice cheese
- Breakfast meat of choice (Canadian bacon, ham, bacon, turkey sausage, or turkey bacon)

Instructions

1. Toast english muffin
2. Scramble egg
3. Cook breakfast meat of choice
4. Place cheese slice on egg for 15-20 seconds
5. Assemble the sandwich
6. Season with salt and pepper to taste

Nutrition Information Per Serving

Nutrition facts vary based on desired breakfast meat.

French Toast

 Prep Time:
5 Minutes

 Cook Time:
5-10 Minutes

 Total Time:
10-15 Minutes

Servings:
2

Dietitian Pro Tip:

This is a healthy twist to your standard french toast recipe by switching to whole wheat bread. Whole wheat bread is higher in fiber, which will slow down digestion and help keep us full longer! Pair with an egg for a balanced breakfast!

Ingredients

- 4 slices whole wheat bread
- 3 eggs
- 1 cup unsweetened vanilla almond milk
- 1 tsp butter

Instructions

1. Crack eggs into bowl
2. Whisk eggs with almond milk
3. Melt butter in frying pan on low heat
4. Soak bread in egg mixture on both sides
5. Place bread in frying pan with a fork
6. Cook until golden brown

Nutrition Information Per Serving

Calories: 259, Total Fat: 12g, Total Carbohydrates: 23g, Protein: 16g

Strawberries and Cream Smoothie

 Prep Time:
2 Minutes

Servings:
1

Dietitian Pro Tip:

Are you looking for a way to sneak veggies into your kid's meals? Frozen riced cauliflower is a great way to add vegetables for breakfast and give the smoothie a creamy texture without changing the flavor or the color!

Ingredients

- 2/3 cup frozen strawberries
- 1/3 cup frozen riced cauliflower
- 1 cup low sugar strawberry greek yogurt
- 1/2 cup milk
- 1/2 scoop ascent strawberry

Instructions

1. Add all ingredients to the blender
2. Mix until smooth
3. Enjoy!

Breakfast

Nutrition Information Per Serving

Calories: 260, Total Fat: 4g, Total Carbohydrates: 27g, Protein: 27g

Blueberry Lemon Ricotta Pancakes

 Prep Time: 10 Minutes

 Cook Time: 15 Minutes

 Total Time: 25 Minutes

Servings: 20

Dietitian Pro Tip:

Pancakes are usually high in sugar and low in protein, but this recipe is different! Refreshing from the lemon zest and added protein from the collagen, these pancakes make a balanced breakfast that will keep you and your little ones full! Collagen protein is excellent for cooking because it doesn't change the consistency or the flavor of the food.

Ingredients

- 1 1/2 cups whole milk
- 3/4 cup whole milk ricotta cheese
- 2 large eggs
- 2 tbsps salted butter, melted
- 2 tbsps agave
- 2 tsps vanilla extract
- 2 tbsps lemon zest
- 1 1/2 cups white whole wheat flour or all-purpose flour

- 2 tsps baking powder
- 1 tsp salt
- 2 scoops Bubs collagen protein powder (or collagen protein of choice)
- 1 1/2 cups fresh or frozen blueberries

Instructions

1. In a large mixing bowl, whisk the wet ingredients together (whole milk, ricotta, eggs, butter, agave, vanilla, and lemon zest)

2. Stir in the flour, baking powder, Bubs Collagen protein, and salt

3. If the batter feels a little too thin, add 1/4 cup additional flour

4. Fold in the blueberries.

5. Allow the batter to sit for 5 minutes

6. Heat a large skillet or griddle over medium heat and add a little butter, or spray with cooking spray

7. Pour about 1/4 cup pancake batter onto the center of the hot pan.

8. Cook until bubbles appear on the surface

9. Using a spatula, gently flip the pancake over and cook the other side for a minute, or until golden

10. Repeat with the remaining batter.

11. Makes about 20 pancakes

Nutrition Information Per Serving
Calories: 96, Total Fat: 3.5g, Total Carbohydrates: 11g, Protein: 5g

Avocado Egg Cups

 Prep Time:
10 Minutes

 Cook Time:
18 Minutes

Total Time:
28 Minutes

Servings:
4

Dietitian Pro Tip:

These avocado egg cups are absolutely scrumptious and so much fun to make. Get the entire family in the kitchen to help prepare this recipe.

Ingredients

- 2 avocados
- 4 medium eggs
- Salt and pepper to taste
- Favorite egg toppings:
    - Chopped basil and tomato
    - Peppers and cheddar cheese
    - 1 ounce sliced ham and cheese

Instructions

1. Preheat oven to 425 °F

2. Cut avocado in half

3. Remove the seed

4. With a spoon, remove 1-2 tablespoons of the inside of the avocado to make room for the egg

5. In a measuring cup, crack one medium egg

6. Pour the egg into the avocado

7. Top with salt, pepper and your favorite toppings

8. Repeat for the other 3 avocado halves

9. Bake for 18 minutes or until whites are cooked all the way through

Shout out to Ashley Osterman, our Director of Nutrition Education at Healthy Steps Nutrition, for all of your help creating recipes, adding the dietitian tips and creating the awesome bonuses to go along with this cookbook that can be found at **healthystepsnutrition.com/cookbook**

Nutrition Information Per Serving

Calories: 153, Total Fat: 12g, Total Carbohydrates: 5g, Protein: 7g

Main Dishes

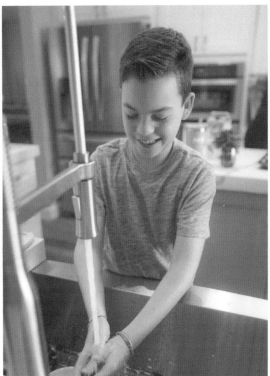

Meatloaf Muffins

 Prep Time: 15 Minutes

 Cook Time: 20 Minutes

 Total Time: 35 Minutes

Servings: 10-12

Dietitian Pro Tip:

Perfectly portioned and a delicious source of protein. If you are looking to add a little flavor (and fat), use one package of lean sirloin and one package of 99% fat free ground turkey. Meatloaf muffins are great reheated.

Ingredients

- 1 pound 99% fat free ground turkey
- 1 pound 90% fat free ground turkey or ground sirloin
- 2 eggs
- 1 packet low sodium McCormick Meatloaf Mix
- 1/3 cup chopped veggies (celery, peppers, onions)
- 1/3 cup panko

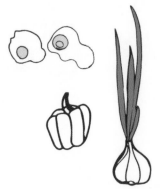

Main Dishes

Instructions

1. Preheat oven to 375 °F

2. Mix all ingredients together

3. Evenly proportion into muffin pan (makes 10-12) and bake for 18-22 minutes

Nutrition Information Per Serving
Calories: 120, Total Fat:4g, Total Carbohydrates: 5g, Protein: 18g

Pecan Crusted Chicken

 Prep Time:
10 Minutes

 Cook Time:
45 Minutes

 Total Time:
55 Minutes

Servings:
6

Dietitian Pro Tip:

Pecan crusted chicken is a great way to add healthy fat to a lean protein source! Don't like pecans? Try using almond slivers or macadamia nuts instead.

Ingredients

- 2 pounds organic chicken breasts
- 1/2 cup spicy brown mustard
- 2 tbsps organic honey
- 1 cup pecans

Instructions

1. Preheat oven to 350 °F
2. In a mixing bowl, whisk together honey and mustard
3. Place pecans in food processer and pulse until the nuts are finely chopped

Instructions

4. Pour chopped pecans in a large mixing bowl

5. Trim fat off chicken breasts

6. Remove any excess moisture from the chicken breasts with a paper towel

7. Coat chicken breast with mustard-honey mixture then place in the chopped pecan bowl

8. Coat the chicken breast with pecans

9. Place crusted chicken breasts in glass baking dish and bake for 25 minutes

Nutrition Information Per Serving

Calories: 280, Total Fat: 13g,
Total Carbohydrates: 8g,
Protein: 27g

Pairs great with Roasted Broccoli on page 72 or Veggie Quinoa on page 86.

Panko Crusted Chicken

 Prep Time:
5 Minutes

 Cook Time:
15 Minutes

Total Time:
20 Minutes

 Servings:
4

Dietitian Pro Tip:

Think healthy alternative to a fried chicken tender. Looking for a crispier texture? Try cooking in the air fryer: 350 °F for 12 minutes (shake and flip about 7 minutes in).

Ingredients

- 1 pound organic chicken breasts
- 2/3 cup panko
- 1 egg
- 1/2 tsp salt
- 1/4 tsp pepper

Main Dishes

Instructions

1. Preheat oven to 375 °F

2. Whisk egg

3. Trim fat on chicken breast then cut into 2 inch strips

4. Mix panko, salt and pepper in a zip-lock bag

5. Coat baking sheet with non-stick spray

6. Place chicken in egg wash then toss in the panko mixture

7. Place on a baking sheet

8. Cook for 15-20 minutes

Nutrition Information Per Serving

Calories: 160, Total Fat: 3g, Total Carbohydrates: 5g, Protein: 28g

Turkey Sausage Bolognese

 Prep Time: 20 Minutes

 Cook Time: 20 Minutes

 Total Time: 40 Minutes

Servings: 8

Dietitian Pro Tip:

When cooking for the family, you don't want to feel like a short-order cook. At Healthy Steps Nutrition, we teach families to make a staple protein and change the sides for parents and kids. This recipe could easily be turned into a lower carbohydrate option when paired with zoodles or spaghetti squash. To add carbohydrates, pair it with whole wheat pasta.

Ingredients

- 2 tbsps olive oil
- (1) 12oz jar roasted red peppers coarsely chopped
- 2 tbsps Italian Parsely coarsely chopped
- 2 1/2 pounds Turkey or Chicken Sausage (hot or mild) REMOVE CASING
- (1) 12oz jar/can artichoke hearts drained and diced
- (1) 8oz jar sun-dried tomato pesto

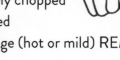

- 1/2 tsp black pepper
- (1) 5oz container plain Greek yogurt
- 4 oz heavy whipping cream
- 4-6 garlic cloves finely chopped
- 2 large tomatoes coarsely chopped

Instructions

1. Remove sausage casing: Cut almost in half lengthwise (butterfly); turn sausage over and peel casing away
2. Pre-heat large skillet with 2 tbsps of olive oil over medium heat and cook turkey sausage while breaking it apart
3. Drain excess grease and place meat back in pan
4. Stir in garlic, peppers, tomatoes, pesto, and artichokes and cook approx. 3-4 minutes over medium heat
5. In a separate bowl, mix the yogurt and heavy whipping cream.
6. Add the liquid mix to the pan and stir over low-medium heat for approx. 3-4 minutes or until thickens.
7. Stir in pepper and parsley
8. Serve over spaghetti squash
9. *Optional sprinkle shredded parmesan over top

Nutrition Information Per Serving
Calories: 420, Total Fat: 24g, Total Carbohydrates: 23g, Protein: 27g

Mexican Fiesta Bowl

 Prep Time:
20 Minutes

 Cook Time:
20 Minutes

 Total Time:
40 Minutes

Servings:
3

> **Dietitian Pro Tip:**
> Fiesta bowls are a fun recipe that allows kids of all ages to get involved in the kitchen. Portion out the rice, beans, and protein, then let them add their toppings. To create a balanced meal, don't forget your veggies! We love sauteed peppers, onions, and mushrooms and starting the bowl with chopped lettuce on the bottom. Remember, rice and beans are both carbohydrates, so together, they should equal about 1/4 of your plate or about one cup.

Ingredients

- 1/2 cup brown rice cooked
- 1 cup black beans drained and rinsed
- 12 oz grilled chicken chopped
- 2 cups bell peppers chopped
- 2 cloves garlic
- 1 tbsp olive oil

Pico

- 4-6 plum tomatoes
- 1/2 freshly squeezed limes
- 1/2 a red onion
- 1/4 cup chopped fresh cilantro
- 1 tsp salt
- 1 tsp pepper

Instructions

1. Sauté peppers, onion, and garlic in olive oil

2. Combine sautéed veggies with rice, black beans, and grilled chicken

3. Fresh Pico: Mix ingredients together (chopped tomatoes, chopped onions, salt, pepper, chopped cilantro and lime juice)

4. Divide mixture into 3 servings

5. Top with 1/3 avocado per bowl

Nutrition Information Per Serving

Calories: 420, Total Fat: 16g, Total Carbohydrates: 38g, Protein: 32g

Crockpot Chili

 Prep Time:
15 Minutes

 Cook Time:
4 Hours

 Total Time:
4 hours 15
Minutes

Servings:
8

Dietitian Pro Tip:

By switching to a lean ground turkey instead of ground beef, you will cut the fat content and create a more balanced meal. We will pair this with mini corn muffins because you can't have traditional chili without corn muffins and roasted veggies!

Ingredients

- 2 pounds 93% lean ground turkey
- 2 packets chili seasoning
- 1 whole red or orange bell pepper, diced
- 1 whole jalapeno, minced (with seeds for heat)
- 1/2 onion diced
- 2 14oz cans diced tomatoes of your choice (we like fire roasted)
- 2 cups water
- 1-2 cloves garlic, minced
- 1 tsp black pepper
- 1 tsp salt
- 1 14oz can chili beans or red beans (rinse the beans from can with water)

Instructions

1. In a large skillet, brown ground turkey until it is cooked.
2. Strain grease and place back in pan
3. Add red or orange pepper, onion, jalapeno, garlic, salt, and pepper
4. Cook over medium heat for 3-4 minutes

Main Dishes

5. Place all ingredients from skillet into crockpot

6. Add canned tomatoes, water, and chili seasoning and stir well

7. Cook in covered crockpot on high for 4 hours or low for 8 hours

8. Approximately 10 minutes before serving, add beans to mix

Nutrition Information Per Serving
Calories: 260, Total Fat: 9g, Total Carbohydrates: 19g, Protein: 28g

White Bean Chicken Chili

 Prep Time: 20 Minutes

 Cook Time: 8 Hours

 Total Time: 8 hours 20 Minutes

Servings: 8

Dietitian Pro Tip:

Even though it is rarely cold enough in South Florida for "chili weather," Brody and Cooper love having this recipe! White chicken chili is a hearty crockpot chili recipe loaded with protein and is excellent reheated. This recipe would be great for a ski trip where you can prep in the morning and set it, then forget it. Pair with veggies for a balanced meal.

Ingredients

- 1 whole onion chopped
- 2-3 cloves garlic, minced
- (1) 14.5 oz can reduced sodium chicken broth
- 1 jar salsa verde
- (1) 14.5 oz can reduced sodium diced tomatoes
- (1) 4.5 oz can diced green chilies
- 1 1/2 tsps chili powder
- 1/2 tsp dried oregano
- 1 tsp ground cumin
- 1/2 tsp salt
- (2) 15 oz can corn kernels, drain and rinsed
- (2) 15 oz can white beans, cannellini, drain and rinse
- 4 large organic chicken breasts approximately 2-2.5 pounds

Making the Roux

- 3 tbsps butter
- 3 tbsps almond flour
- 1/2 cup reduced fat milk
- 4 oz heavy whipping cream
- 1 tsp chicken bouilon
- 1 tsp black pepper
- 5 oz plain Greek yogurt (1 small container)

Instructions

1. Place the 4 raw chicken breasts in the bottom of the crockpot, cover with all of the spices on top, then throw in the rest of the ingredients before the cream base roux

2. Cook on low 6-8 hours.

3. One hour before serving, melt the butter in a saucepan over medium heat, slowly whisk in the flour and allow it to bubble and brown a little (approx. 3-5 minutes)

4. Next, whisk in milk, cream, chicken bullion, yogurt, and black pepper and let simmer another 4-5 minutes

5. Pour roux mixture into crockpot.

6. Shred the chicken with two forks and allow the sauce to thicken while cooking on low for another hour.

7. It may be easier to remove the chicken and shred over a pan or plate and then place back in crockpot

8. Additional toppings not listed could be: cilantro, cheese, hot sauce or tortilla strips (nutrition facts not included for toppings)

9. Enjoy our favorite winter chicken chili recipe! Servings are based off of 350 grams each

Nutrition Information Per Serving

Calories: 390, Total Fat: 12g, Total Carbohydrates: 51g, Protein: 21g

Turkey Burgers

 Prep Time: 15 Minutes

 Cook Time: 15 Minutes

 Total Time: 30 Minutes

Servings: 12

Dietitian Pro Tip:

Do your turkey burgers taste bland and dried out? If so, this is a recipe you need to try! Turkey burgers are lower in fat, which means they will dry out easier when cooking. The fresh parsley in this recipe gives a fresh flavor. Try putting this turkey burger on a sandwich thin or in-between sweet potato toast. Pair with veggies for a balanced meal.

Ingredients

- 3 pounds 93% lean ground turkey
- 1/4 cup panko breadcrumbs
- 1/4 cup onion finely diced
- 2 egg whites lightly beaten
- 1/4 cup parsley chopped
- 1-2 cloves garlic peeled and minced
- 1 tsp salt
- 1/4 tsp black pepper
- 1/4 cup sun-dried tomatoes minced

Instructions

1. In a large bowl, mix ground turkey, panko, onion, egg whites, parsley, garlic, salt, pepper, and sun dried tomatoes

Main Dishes

2. Form into 12 patties. This equates to approximately 12-4oz burgers. (We like to place our patties on wax paper and refrigerate prior to cooking to firm up the patties prior to grilling)

3. Cook the patties in a medium-large size skillet over medium heat, or place on grill turning once, to an internal temperature of 180 °F

4. A note from the Chef: These also double as delicious homemade meatballs with your favorite red sauce

Nutrition Information Per Serving
Calories: 170, Total Fat: 8g, Total Carbohydrates: 2g, Protein: 23g

Herb Encrusted Mustard Salmon

 Prep Time:
10 Minutes

 Cook Time:
8 Minutes

 Total Time:
18 Minutes

Servings:
4

Dietitian Pro Tip:

Salmon is an excellent source of omega-3s, which are essential for brain health and help fight inflammation. Do you find your salmon dried out when you cook it? We love this recipe because the salmon stays moist and the herbs give it such a fresh taste! Pair with roasted broccoli (find the recipe on page 72) and potatoes for a balanced meal.

Ingredients

- (4) 6oz salmon filets
- 2 tbsps grainy Mustard
- 2 cloves garlic, minced
- 1 tbsp shallots, finely minced
- 2 tsps fresh Thyme, chopped plus extra for garnish
- 2 tsps fresh rosemary, chopped
- 1/2 juiced lemon plus a slice each for garnish
- salt & pepper to taste

Instructions

1. Heat oven on broil mode and line a baking sheet with foil
2. In a small bowl, mix together mustard, garlic, shallots, thyme, rosemary, and lemon juice
3. Place salmon on baking sheet and spread the mixture over each piece of salmon.
4. Season to taste with salt and pepper
5. Broil 7-8 minutes

Main Dishes

Nutrition Information Per Serving

Calories: 240, Total Fat: 8g, Total Carbohydrates: 2g, Protein: 38g

Chicken Curry with Roasted Cashews

 Prep Time: 15 Minutes   Cook Time: 15 Minutes   Total Time: 30 Minutes   Servings: 5

Dietitian Pro Tip:
This recipe is not your traditional curry; it's slightly sweet and savory. This recipe is great for leftovers, but it's best to leave the cashews separate, so they don't get soggy.

Ingredients

- 2 pounds chicken breast boneless and skinless
- 1 cup celery, diced
- 1/4 cup chopped green scalllions
- 1/4 cup raisins
- 1/2 cup salted cashews whole or pieces

Sauce

- 1/3 cup white cooking wine
- 1/4 cup mango chutney original or hot
- 3 tbsps curry powder
- 1 cup light mayo

Instructions

1. Season chicken breasts with olive oil, salt, and pepper

2. Cook chicken on the grill until cooked.

3. Dice chicken into small 1 inch pieces

4. Combine chicken, celery, scallions, and raisins together

5. In a separate bowl, mix together wine, chutney, curry powder, and mayo

Main Dishes

4. Pour sauce over chicken mixture

5. Place cashews in a small skillet and cook over medium heat for 3-5 minutes or until roasted to your liking. We recommend keeping the cashews on the side until ready to serve

Nutrition Information Per Serving

Calories: 440, Total Fat: 22g, Total Carbohydrates: 22g, Protein: 40g

BBQ Pulled Chicken

 Prep Time: 10 Minutes

 Cook Time: 6 Hour

 Total Time: 6 hours 10 Minutes

Servings: 6

Dietitian Pro Tip:

BBQ sauce is a hidden source of sugar! Have you ever looked at the nutrition facts for BBQ sauce? Many are loaded with sugar. We love Stubb's BBQ because it has 50% less sugar than traditional BBQ sauces. Next time you use BBQ sauce, check and see how much you use and how much sugar is in each serving. You will be surprised!

Equipment

- Slow Cooker

Ingredients

- 2 pounds organic chicken breasts
- 2/3 cup Stubb's BBQ sauce
- 1/2 cup water
- 1 tbsp brown sugar
- 1/2 tsp chili powder
- 1/2 tsp onion powder
- 1/2 tsp salt
- 1/2 tsp pepper

Instructions

1. Make rub by combining brown sugar, chili powder, onion powder, salt and pepper
2. Rub the seasoning mixture onto the trimmed chicken breasts and place into the crockpot

Main Dishes

3. Pour Stubb's BBQ sauce over the chicken breasts (cover both sides of the breast)
4. Add 1/2 cup water to the crockpot
5. Cook on low for 6 hours
6. Shred with a fork

Nutrition Information Per Serving
Calories: 160, Total Fat: 2g, Total Carbohydrates: 6g, Protein: 29g

Pulled Chicken with Salsa Verde

 Prep Time: 10 Minutes

 Cook Time: 6 Hours

 Total Time: 6 Hours 10 Minutes

 Servings: 5

Dietitian Pro Tip:

This recipe is a staple in the Aucoin household and the kid's favorite way to cook chicken! There are so many different ways you can use this recipe. Here are a few ideas: tacos, Mexican bowls, stuffed sweet potatoes, or a salad.

Ingredients

- 4 chicken breasts
- (1) 12-ounce jar of salsa verde
- 1 packet taco seasoning

Instructions

1. Rinse chicken breasts and lay in the bottom of the crockpot

2. Sprinkle taco seasoning on both sides of the chicken breast

3. Pour jar of salsa verde over the chicken breasts

4. Cook on low for 6 hours in the crockpot

5. Shred with two forks

Nutrition Information Per Serving

Calories: 160, Total Fat: 2g, Total Carbohydrates: 6g, Protein: 29g

Sloppy Joe's

 Prep Time:
15 Minutes

 Cook Time:
20 Minutes

 Total Time:
35 Minutes

Servings:
8

Dietitian Pro Tip:

This sloppy joe is a family favorite! Are you looking for an easy recipe to bring to a BBQ or a family function? Premake this recipe then reheat it in the crockpot. Best served on a potato roll. Pair it with sweet potato toast and roasted veggies for a lower carb option.

Ingredients

- 2 pounds organic ground beef 90/10
- 1 white/sweet onion diced
- 2 bell peppers diced red, green, orange or yellow
- 5 cloves garlic minced
- 1 1/4 cups organic ketchup
- 2 tbsps organic honey
- 2 tsps chili powder
- 1 tsp dry mustard
- 1/2 tsp red pepper flakes
- 1 1/2 tbsps worcestershire sauce
- 2 tbsps organic tomato paste
- 3 tbsps salted butter
- 1 tbsp Dijon mustard
- 1 1/2 tsps liquid smoke
- 1/4 cup apple cider vinegar
- 1/2 tsp black pepper
- 1 cup water

Instructions

1. Place 1 tbsp butter and garlic in saute pan and brown the ground beef

2. Drain and keep separate

3. Place tomato paste in saute pan with remaining butter

4. Add onion and bell pepper

5. Saute until vegetables are soft, approx 5 minutes

6. Meanwhile, place all liquid ingredients in a bowl and whisk together

7. Next, add the ground beef mixture back into the onion, tomato paste, and bell peppers

8. Place the remaining dry ingredients into the beef mixture, stir, and then stir in the liquids (including the water)

9. Cook over medium heat until the desired thickness of the sauce is reduced to your liking

Cooper's Favorite

Nutrition Information Per Serving
Calories: 330, Total Fat: 16g,
Total Carbohydrates: 22g,
Protein: 24g

Egg Roll in a Bowl

 Prep Time: 15 Minutes

 Cook Time: 15 Minutes

 Total Time: 30 Minutes

Servings: 3

Dietitian Pro Tip:

This recipe is not only delicious but it is super easy! Only 3 ingredients and no prep needed! Pair this recipe with roasted sweet potato or brown rice for a healthy balanced meal.

Ingredients

- 1 pound 97% lean ground turkey
- 16 oz bag tri-color coleslaw mix (453 grams) green cabbage, red cabbage, and carrots
- 1/4 cup coconut aminos (or low sodium tamari or soy sauce)

Instructions

1. Brown ground turkey in large non-stick pan on medium-high heat
2. Once turkey is cooked (about 5-8 minutes) add in shredded coleslaw mix
3. Reduce heat to medium and cook while stirring for another 5 minutes or until cabbage and carrots become tender
4. Add in coconut aminos, stir, and cook for an additional 1-2 minutes
5. Remove from heat and divide into 3 portions
6. *Optional: top with chili sauce, toasted sesame seeds, or shrimp (not included in nutrition facts)

Main Dishes

Nutrition Information Per Serving

Calories: 290, Total Fat: 11g, Total Carbohydrates: 18g, Protein: 31g

Tuna Salad

Prep Time:
10 Minutes

Serving Size:
2

Dietitian Pro Tip:

This recipe is simple and delicious. Turn it into a tuna melt by placing the tuna salad on an English Muffin and a slice of cheese in the toaster oven. Pair with your favorite raw veggies for a balanced meal.

Ingredients

- (1) 4 oz can albacore tuna
- (1) 4 oz can skipjack tuna
- 1 tsp lemon juice
- 2 tbsps mayonnaise
- 2 tbsps finely chopped pickles

- 2 tbsps mayonnaise
- 1 tsp onion powder
- 1 tsp cumin
- Salt and pepper to taste

Instructions

1. Drain the cans of tuna
2. Mix all ingredients together with a fork

Nutrition Information Per Serving

Calories: 280, Total Fat: 15g, Protein: 30g

English Muffin Pizza

 Prep Time:
10 Minutes

 Cook Time:
10 Minutes

Total Time:
20 Minutes

 Servings:
2

Dietitian Pro Tip:

Who doesn't love pizza? English muffin pizzas are a fun one for kids of any age! Make it your own by adding your favorite toppings.
Pro Tip: whole-grain English Muffins are a better fiber source, which slows down digestion and will keep you fuller longer.

Ingredients

- 2 whole wheat english muffins
- 1/4 cup favorite pizza sauce
- 1 cup fresh mozzarella cheese
- Favorite pizza toppings (pepperoni, mushrooms, fresh tomatoes, basil, etc)

Instructions

1. Preheat the oven to 375 °F
2. Cut english muffins in half
3. Top with pizza sauce
4. Top with fresh mozzarella cheese
5. Add your favorite pizza toppings
6. Bake for 10 minutes or until the cheese is melted and browned on the edges

Nutrition Information
Per Serving

Calories: 230, Total Fat: 8g, Total Carbohydrates: 29g, Protein: 13g
Favorite pizza toppings not included in nutrition facts

Balsamic Pulled Pork

 Prep Time: 5 Minutes

 Cook Time: 4 Hours

 Total Time: 4 Hours 5 Minutes

Servings: 4

Dietitian Pro Tip:

Are you looking for a new crockpot dish? This crockpot recipe is lower in fat than your traditional pulled pork but still loaded with flavor! Pair with roasted sweet potatoes and veggies for a balanced meal.

Ingredients

- 1 1/2 pounds boneless pork tenderloin
- 1 cup low sodium chicken broth
- 1/2 cup balsamic vinegar
- 1 tbsp worcestershire sauce
- 1 tbsp low sodium soy sauce
- 1 tbsp organic honey
- 1/2 tsp red pepper flakes
- 2 cloves of garlic (minced)

Instructions

1. Place pork tenderloin into crockpot
2. In a medium mixing bowl, combine all other ingredients (broth, balsamic vinegar, worcestershire sauce, soy sauce, honey, garlic, and pepper flakes) and pour over pork tenderloin
3. Cook for 4 hours on high or 6 hours on low
4. Once pork is done, pull out of crockpot and shred with two forks
5. Use the remaining liquid as gravy

Nutrition Information Per Serving

Calories: 180, Total Fat: 4g, Total Carbohydrates: 11g, Protein: 27g

Main Dishes

Cheesy Beef and Broccoli Bake

 Prep Time:
10 Minutes

 Cook Time:
25 Minutes

Total Time:
35 Minutes

Servings:
4

Dietitian Pro Tip:

This dish is a healthy spin on a Shepherd's Pie. If you have a hard time getting veggies in, this is a recipe to try! Pro tip: cut the broccoli up in small pieces to ensure it cooks thoroughly.

Ingredients

- 1 pound lean ground beef 93/7
- 1 large head broccoli about, 5 cups chopped
- 1 large container frozen garlic mashed cauliflower, about 2.5 cups
- 1/2 cup low fat shredded cheddar cheese
- 1 tsp garlic powder (optional)

Instructions

1. Preheat oven to 400 °F
2. Brown ground beef and season with garlic powder (optional)
3. Warm up the container of frozen mashed cauliflower in the microwave according to package instructions
4. Chop up the head of broccoli
5. Mix browned beef, warmed mashed cauliflower, and chopped broccoli together in a 9x13 baking dish
6. Bake for 20 minutes
7. Remove dish from the oven and sprinkle with shredded cheese
8. Place dish back in oven until cheese has melted (3-5 minutes)

Main Dishes

9. Remove from oven, let cool and enjoy

*Note: you could also use the HSN Garlic Mashed Cauliflower recipe on page 76 in place of store bought

Nutrition Information Per Serving

Calories: 360, Total Fat: 18g, Total Carbohydrates: 19g, Protein: 34g

Side Dishes

Roasted Broccoli

 Prep Time:
5 Minutes

 Cook Time:
20 Minutes

 Total Time:
25 Minutes

Servings:
2

Dietitian Pro Tip:

Roasted broccoli is a staple side dish in our house. We usually enjoy it multiple times a week. Pro tip: wash and chop up your broccoli before you store it in the refrigerator so it is ready to roast!

Ingredients

- 1 large head broccoli (about 5 cups chopped)
- 1 tsp olive oil
- Salt and pepper to taste

Instructions

1. Preheat oven to 400 °F
2. Wash and chop broccoli
3. Mix in olive oil
4. Add salt and pepper to taste
5. Line baking sheet with aluminum foil
6. Bake for 20 minutes

Nutrition Information Per Serving

Calories: 100, Total Fat: 3g, Total Carbohydrates: 15g, Protein: 7g

Cooper's Favorite

Buffalo Cauliflower

 Prep Time:
5 Minutes

 Cook Time:
15 Minutes

 Total Time:
20 Minutes

Servings:
3

Dietitian Pro Tip:

We are huge fans of the air fryer because it makes your food taste crispy without using a ton of oil in a frying pan. This recipe has a kick so if your little ones don't love spicy, save it for the adults. If you are looking for less of a kick, lower the recipe's amount of hot sauce. If you don't have an air fryer, cook in the oven at 375 °F for 30 minutes (broil for the last 2-3 minutes).

Ingredients

- 2 cups raw cauliflower
- 1/2 cup Frank's Hot sauce
- 2 tbsps butter

Instructions

1. Chop cauliflower into small pieces

2. Melt butter in microwave

3. Mix butter and hot sauce

4. Pour liquid over the cauliflower, mix well

5. Cook in air fryer on 360 °F for 15 minutes (or until golden brown)

Nutrition Information Per Serving

Calories: 110, Total Fat: 8g, Total Carbohydrates: 20g, Protein: 3g

 Brody's
Favorite

Side Dishes

Garlic Mashed Cauliflower

 Prep Time: 5 Minutes

 Cook Time: 20 Minutes

Total Time: 25 Minutes

Servings: 2

Dietitian Pro Tip:

Mashed cauliflower is a great alternative to mashed potatoes! If you have a hard time getting veggies in, try this recipe mixed in with mashed potatoes to increase the volume and "sneak" veggies into the meal. Make it your own by topping with cheese or a few bacon crumbles!

Ingredients

- 1 head fresh cauliflower
- 1 cup chicken broth
- 1/4 tsp fresh cracked pepper
- 2 cloves garlic crushed

Instructions

1. Cut your cauliflower head of into small chunks
2. Place all ingredients into a medium saucepan and heat to a boil
3. Reduce heat to medium and cover, and allow to cook for 20 minutes (you may need to add more chicken stock if it dries up)
4. Carefully pour ingredients into blender and blend until smooth

Nutrition Information Per Serving

Calories: 110, Total Fat: 8g, Total Carbohydrates: 20g, Protein: 3g

Yummy Kale Chips

 Prep Time:
2 Minutes

 Cook Time:
15 Minutes

 Total Time:
17 Minutes

Servings:
2

Dietitian Pro Tip:

Kale is often referred to as a superfood because it is an excellent source of vitamin A, K, C, Manganese, Calcium, Potassium, and Magnesium. If you find kale has a bitter taste, this recipe might be the way for you to enjoy it. Kale chips are best fresh out of the oven!

Ingredients

- 3 cups kale
- 3 tsps olive oil
- 1/2 tsp salt

Instructions

1. Preheat oven to 350 °F

2. Line large baking sheet with aluminum foil

3. Spread 3 cups kale on baking sheet

4. Drizzle with olive oil and sea salt

5. Bake for 15-18 minutes

Nutrition Information Per Serving

Calories: 140, Total Fat: 8g, Total Carbohydrates: 13g, Protein: 6g

Honey Sriracha Brussels

 Prep Time:
5 Minutes

 Cook Time:
15 Minutes

Total Time:
20 Minutes

Servings:
2

> **Dietitian Pro Tip:**
>
> If you are looking for an easy way to make crispy brussels sprouts that taste delicious, this is a recipe you must try! This recipe is sweet with a little kick. Brussel sprouts are an excellent source of vitamin C. Pair with protein and starch for a balanced meal.

Equipment

- Air Fryer

Ingredients

- 2 cups brussel sprouts
- 1 tbsp honey
- 2 tbsps sriracha
- 1 spray olive oil

Instructions

1. Rinse and dry brussel sprouts

2. Cut brussel sprouts in half then lightly coat them with a spray of olive oil

3. Mix honey and sriracha together then toss the brussel sprouts in the mixture

4. Place brussel sprouts in air fryer and cook at 350 °F for 15 minutes (shake the basket every 4-5 minutes)

5. Remove from air fryer and divide into two portions

6. Chop up cooked bacon slices and sprinkle over the top

Nutrition Information Per Serving

Calories: 120, Total Fat: 4g, Total Carbohydrates: 18g, Protein: 6g

Spaghetti Squash

 Prep Time: 5 Minutes

 Cook Time: 30-35 Minutes

 Total Time: 35-40 Minutes

Servings: 5

Dietitian Pro Tip:

Spaghetti squash is one of those veggies that most people have heard about but have never tried because they are unsure how to cook it. We love making spaghetti squash paired with red sauce and ground meat for the adults. For the kids, you can mix spaghetti squash with whole wheat pasta to sneak in veggies.

Fun fact: one cup of spaghetti squash contains 10 grams of carbohydrates, while one cup of your standard pasta contains 43 grams of carbohydrates.

Ingredients

- 1 medium spaghetti squash (about 4 pounds)
- 1 tsp olive oil
- 1 pinch salt

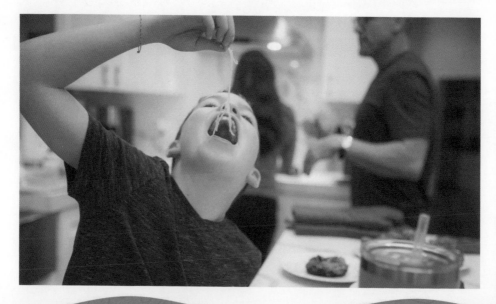

Instructions

1. Heat oven to 400 °F
2. Slice squash in half lengthwise and scoop out seeds
3. Drizzle halves with olive oil
4. Season with salt
5. Place squash cut side down on baking sheet and roast until tender (about 30-35 minutes)
5. Use a fork to scrape out "spaghetti" squash

Nutrition Information Per Serving
Calories: 60, Total Fat: 2g, Total Carbohydrates: 11g, Protein: 1g

Cinnamon Roasted Butternut Squash

 Prep Time: 5 Minutes

 Cook Time: 20 Minutes

 Total Time: 25 Minutes

Servings: 2

Dietitian Pro Tip:

Cinnamon hits the same taste buds as sugar, so it gives you a sweet flavor without the added sugar! You can follow these exact instructions with sweet potato to make roasted sweet potatoes, which are also delicious! Sweet potato and butternut squash are considered starchy veggies. If you follow the plate method, this squash recipe will comprise 1/4 of your plate, while non-starchy veggies will make up half of your plate. Pair with roasted broccoli (non-starchy veggie) and protein for a balanced meal. Don't have time to chop the butternut squash? You can purchase pre-cut cubes of butternut squash which cuts the prep time down significantly! That's what we do!

Ingredients

- 1 1/3 cups butternut squash peeled and cut into cubes
- 1 tsp olive oil
- 2/3 tsp ground cinnamon
- 1/2 tsp kosher salt
- Optional: dash cayenne

Instructions

1. Preheat oven to 425 °F
2. Place aluminum foil on one large baking sheet
3. Mix the cinnamon and salt together
4. Toss the butternut squash cubes into the olive oil then in the seasoning mixture until they are coated well
5. Place coated butternut squash on the baking sheet in a thin layer (spread out evenly on baking sheet)
6. Place baking sheet in the oven
7. Flip the squash after 20-25 minutes
8. Cook for about 40-45 minutes total (until edges are lightly brown and the centers are tender)

Nutrition Information Per Serving

Calories: 87, Total Fat: 2g, Total Carbohydrates: 17g, Protein: 2g

Veggie Quinoa

 Prep Time:
5 Minutes

 Cook Time:
20 Minutes

 Total Time:
25 Minutes

Servings:
4

Dietitian Pro Tip:

Veggie quinoa is a great way to get in healthy veggies and a high fiber starch option! Pair this recipe with roasted veggies and pecan-crusted chicken for a balanced meal.

Ingredients

- 2 cups quinoa
- 4 cups low sodium chicken broth
- 2 cups mushrooms chopped
- 1 bag spinach chopped

Instructions

1. Place quinoa and low sodium chicken broth into a medium size pot

2. Heat to a boil then reduce to a simmer and cover

3. Let cook for 15-20 minutes

4. Pour olive oil and mushrooms into a large sauce pan

5. Sauté mushrooms for about 5-7 minutes

6. Pour in the bag of spinach and let cook for an additional 4-5 minutes

7. Mix the veggies in with the quinoa and let sit for 3-4 minutes

8. Portion into 1/2 cup servings

Nutrition Information Per Serving

Calories: 360, Total Fat: 5g, Total Carbohydrates: 64g, Protein: 17g

Treats

Chocolate Chip Protein Cookies

 Prep Time:
5 Minutes

 Cook Time:
8 Minutes

 Total Time:
13 Minutes

Servings:
20

Dietitian Pro Tip:

Who doesn't love cookies?! These are a great low-sugar option for a healthy treat! If you are getting your kids started in the kitchen, this is a great recipe to try.

Ingredients

- 2 cups old fashioned oats
- 2 1/2 scoops Ascent chocolate protein powder
- 1 egg
- 1 tbsp vanilla extract
- 4 tsps semi-sweet chocolate morsels
- 5 tbsps butter
- 1 tsp baking soda
- 2 tbsps agave
- 2 tsps raw sugar cane
- 1/4 tsp salt

Instructions

1. Preheat 350 °F

2. Mix all ingredients

3. Spoon out 20 cookies

4. Bake for 8 minutes

Nutrition Information Per Serving

Calories: 70, Total Fat: 4g, Total Carbohydrates: 5g, Protein: 4g

Brody's Favorite

Peanut Butter Chocolate Smoothie

 Total Time:
5 Minutes

Servings:
1 smoothie or
6 smoothie pops

Dietitian Pro Tip:

One of our favorite treats is a Reese's Peanut Butter Cup. This recipe is a healthy alternative that could be a breakfast smoothie (for an adult) or a refreshing treat in the afternoon. This is also a great way to "sneak" in veggies to your child's diet for those picky eaters.

Ingredients

- 1 cup unsweetened almond milk
- 1 medium sized banana
- 1 cup frozen riced cauliflower
- 1 scoop Chocolate Ascent Protein
- 1 tbsp creamy peanut butter

Instructions

1. Place all ingredients into a blender and blend until smooth
2. Drink as a smoothie or place equally into 6 pop molds

Nutrition Information Per Serving

Calories: 380, Total Fat: 12g, Total Carbohydrates: 40g, Protein: 33g

Treats

Air Fried Apple Slices

 Prep Time:
5 Minutes

 Cook Time:
20 Minutes

 Total Time:
25 Minutes

Servings:
3-4

Dietitian Pro Tip:

These apple crisps are great dipped in vanilla yogurt mixed with cinnamon. We love this afternoon treat that's not loaded with added sugar.

Ingredients

- 2 honey crisp apples
- 1/2 cup coconut flour
- 1/2 teaspoon cinnamon
- Coconut oil spray

Instructions

1. Peel and core the apple

2. Cut into 10-12 slices

3. Spray with coconut oil

4. Combine flour and cinnamon

5. Coat apple slices with flour and cinnamon

6. Bake in air fryer for 10 minutes at 350 °F then flip apple slices

7. Bake for another 10 minutes at 350 °F, shaking every 5 minutes

Nutrition Information Per Serving

Nutrition facts vary based on apple slices.

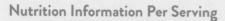

Strawberry Shortcake Smoothie or Smoothie Pops

 Total Time:
5 Minutes

Servings:
1 smoothie or
6 smoothie pops

Dietitian Pro Tip:

Did you like having strawberry shortcake ice cream bars as a kid? This is a healthy alternative that both you and your kids will enjoy! This recipe makes a great breakfast smoothie or refreshing smoothie pops!

Ingredients

- 1 cup almond milk
- 1/2 cup sliced strawberries
- 1 cup frozen riced cauliflower
- 2 heaping tbsps raw cashews
- A splash of vanilla extract
- 1/4 tsp lemon zest
- 1 scoop Ascent strawberry protein powder

Instructions

1. Blend all ingredients together and enjoy

* Makes 1 smoothie or 6 smoothie pops

Nutrition Information Per Serving

Calories: 300, Total Fat: 7g, Total Carbohydrates: 21g, Protein: 31g

Cooper's Favorite

Snacks

Energy Balls

 Prep Time:
5 Minutes

 Total Time:
25 Minutes

Servings:
12

Dietitian Pro Tip:

This recipe is a great on-the-go snack option and sure to be a hit with the whole family! Many convenient bars are not balanced with protein, carbohydrates, and healthy fat. This ball is balanced with protein, carbs, and fat to keep you and your family fueled and energized! Energy balls are a great option to prepare and bring with you to meets and tournaments.

Ingredients

- 1 cup old-fashioned oats
- 4 tbsps almond butter
- 3 tbsps unsweetened applesauce
- 2 tbsps chia seeds
- 2 tbsps dry roasted cocoa nibs
- 3 scoops Ascent whey protein

Instructions

1. Mix all ingredients together

2. If too dry, add a small drop of water to moisten

3. Refrigerate for 15-20 minutes

4. Remove and make into 12 balls

Nutrition Information Per Serving
   Calories: 110, Total Fat: 5g, Total Carbohydrates: 8g, Protein: 9g

Oven Roasted Chickpeas

 Prep Time:
5 Minutes

 Cook Time:
15 Minutes

 Total Time:
20 Minutes

Servings:
4

Dietitian Pro Tip:

This crunchy and savory roasted snack it a great alternative to chips. Plus it is a good source of fiber and protein.

Ingredients

- (1) 15.5 oz can chickpeas
- 1/2 tsp extra virgin olive oil
- 1 tsp garlic powder
- 1/2 tsp salt
- 1/2 tsp onion powder
- 1/4 tsp cayenne pepper

Instructions

1. Preheat oven to 400 °F and line a large rimmed baking sheet with parchment paper
2. Pour rinsed beans onto towel/paper towels and place another towel on top and gently rub until completely dry
3. Transfer to baking sheet
4. Drizzle chickpeas with oil and roll them around until evenly coated
5. Sprinkle with garlic and onion powder, salt, and cayenne
6. Roll them around until evenly coated
7. Roast for 20 minutes and then shake the pan gently to roll the chickpeas around.
8. Roast for 10-15 minutes more, until golden and lightly charred (be sure to keep an eye on them so they don't burn)

Nutrition Information Per Serving

Calories: 100, Total Fat: 2g, Total Carbohydrates: 16g, Protein: 5g

Turkey and Avocado Roll-Ups with Strawberries

 Total Time:
5 Minutes

Servings:
1

> **Dietitian Pro Tip:**
>
> Looking for an easy and balanced snack that the kids can help make? Try these roll-ups! They are easy, and you can have everything prepared then get the kids involved with the assembly. We love adding avocado to roll-ups to give it a creamy flavor while adding healthy fat. For a balanced snack, pair roll-ups with your favorite fruit.

Ingredients

- 1/4 avocado
- 2 ounces turkey
- 1 cup strawberries

Instructions

1. Cut 1/4 avocado into slices
2. Lay out turkey slices
3. Add 1-2 avocado slices to the turkey and roll it up
4. Repeat for the other turkey slices
5. Pair with strawberries for a balanced snack

Nutrition Information Per Serving

Calories: 169, Total Fat: 6g, Total Carbohydrates: 16g, Protein: 15g

Apple Sandwich with Peanut Butter

 Total Time:
5 Minutes

Servings:
1

Dietitian Pro Tip:

Are you looking to get kids involved with snack time? This recipe is a great option! We put a little spin on apples and peanut butter by adding cinnamon. Did you know that cinnamon hits the same taste buds as sugar? This means when you add cinnamon, you think it is sweeter without the added sugar! We love adding cinnamon to oatmeal, bars, pancakes, apples... pretty much anything!

Ingredients

- 1 medium apple
- 3 tsps whipped peanut butter
- Cinnamon

Instructions

1. De-core apple
2. Cup apple in 6 slices
3. Spread 1 tsp of peanut butter on three of the apple slices
4. Sprinkle cinnamon
5. Place plain apple slices on top of the apple slices with peanut butter
6. Enjoy!

Nutrition Information Per Serving

Calories: 155, Total Fat: 6g, Total Carbohydrates: 25g, Protein: 3g

Turkey, Cheese and Cucumber Roll-Up with Strawberries

 Total Time:
5 Minutes

 Servings:
1

> **Dietitian Pro Tip:**
> This roll-up recipe has a little crunch from the cucumber! It's a fun way to sneak veggies into your kid's snacks. Don't like cucumbers? Try shredded carrots instead. We use spreadable cheese split between two roll-ups for this recipe, but you could also use thin-sliced cheese to make two roll-ups. Pair with your favorite fruit for a balanced snack.

Ingredients

- 2 ounces turkey slices
- 1/8 cucumber
- 1 baby bell cheese (21g)
- 1 cup strawberries

Instructions

1. Cut cucumbers in half
2. Cut halves in fourths lengthwise
3. Lay out 2 turkey slices
4. Spread cheese between two slices
5. Add cucumber slice to each turkey slice
5. Roll-up to create a crunchy and delicious snack
5. Pair with strawberries for a balanced snack

Nutrition Information Per Serving

Calories: 169, Total Fat: 7g, Total Carbohydrates: 13g, Protein: 19g

Almond Joy Energy Balls

 Total Time:
10 Minutes

Servings:
12

Dietitian Pro Tip:
These Almond Joy Energy Balls bring chocolate, coconut, and almond together to create a delicious and nutritious bite-sized snack. If you love Almond Joy candy bars, you will love these healthy little energy bites!

Ingredients

- 1 cup old fashioned rolled oats
- 1/2 cup unsweetened shredded coconut
- 1/2 cup creamy almond butter
- 2 scoops Bubs collagen protein
- 2 tsps mini chocolate chips
- 2 tbsps honey

Instructions

1. Mix all ingredients together thoroughly and roll into 12 small balls

2. Place into an airtight container and refrigerate until ready to eat

Nutrition Information Per Serving
Calories: 130, Total Fat: 8g, Total Carbohydrates: 11g, Protein: 5g

Healthy Steps
Nutrition Resources

Free Menu Planning Guide

Are you looking for ideas on how to make balanced meals using Healthy Steps Nutrition recipes? The nutrition experts at Healthy Steps Nutrition work with families individually to create customized plans just for them.

You can get an idea of how to create balanced meals using this free guide at healthystepsnutrition.com/cookbook

Additional Recipes

Did you love these recipes? You can find even more recipes on our website. There are new kid approved and family friendly recipes added regularly!

Find new recipes at healthystepsnutrition.com/healthy-recipes

Individual Nutrition Coaching

Are you looking for a sustainable plan to help you see lasting results? At Healthy Steps Nutrition, we believe something as fundamental as nutrition shouldn't be complicated, which is why we work with clients individually to create a customized plan using a simple, habit-based approach. The nutrition experts at Healthy Steps Nutrition have worked with over 30,000 people worldwide to create a healthy lifestyle one step at a time.

Sign up to work with the experts at healthystepsnutrition.com/coaching

Family Nutrition Programs

Are you looking for individualized support for the whole family? Healthy Steps Nutrition has family nutrition programs.

Learn how your family can work with the experts at healthystepsnutrition.com/family-nutrition-program